James McNeill Whistler

Detail from Plate V.

Funk & Wagnalls, Inc., New York

ANDREW McLAREN YOUNG
RICHMOND PROFESSOR OF FINE ART, UNIVERSITY OF GLASGOW

James McNeill Whistler 1834-1903

James McNeill Whistler (the 'McNeill' was Whistler's own substitution for a baptismal 'Abbott') was born in Lowell, Massachusetts, on July 11, 1834, the son of a U.S. Army engineer and his second wife, Anna McNeill from North Carolina. In 1843 the family moved to St. Petersburg, where Major Whistler was employed by the czar as civil engineer on the railway to Moscow. James's early interest in art was given encouragement both in Russia, through drawing lessons from an officer named Karitzky, and in London during visits to a sister married to Francis Seymour Haden, who was later to become well-known as an etcher. After his father's death in 1849, James, his mother and his younger brother returned to America. In 1851 he entered the U.S. Military Academy at West Point; though he did well at French and drawing, his lack of interest in everything else was the cause of his discharge in 1854. After a few months with the Coast Geodetic Survey in Washington, where he gained useful experience in the technique of etching, he left for Paris resolved to become an artist.

During a period of earnest bohemianism Whistler attended classes at Gleyre's academy and, like other progressive artists of his generation, became interested in Velázquez and in Dutch seventeenth-century painting. In 1858, while copying in the Louvre, he met Fantin-Latour, who introduced him to the avant-garde circle of Courbet. Both before and after this meeting, Courbet's Realism made a great impact on his art.

In 1859 he moved to London where his first major picture, At the Piano (Plate I), was acclaimed and sold. He began by painting and etching the Thames and London's dockside, but soon contact with Rossetti and Pre-Raphaelitism generated an interest in greater aestheticism. In 1864 his enthusiasm for Japanese prints and Chinese porcelain resulted in the inclusion of an increasing number of Oriental accessories in his pictures. In 1865 he was at Trouville with Courbet and, though they remained good friends, this renewed association had the effect of strengthening Whistler's resolve to go his own way as an artist. In 1866, he visited Chile, then in the process of revolution; Symphony in Grey and Green: the Ocean (Plate VI) and a few other sea-scapes are by-products of the journey.

The later 1860's were years of indecisive experiment, with Greek as well as Oriental elements being brought into his work. He emphasized his rejection of Realism by adopting musical or abstract titles for his pictures, calling them 'Symphonies', 'Harmonies' and so on. He also took to signing them with a butterfly emblem elaborated out of his monogram. In the 1870's self-assurance returned: a succession of deliberately composed portraits, called 'Arrangements', and moonlit Thames-side landscapes, or 'Nocturnes', are among his greatest achievements. In this, for him, very fertile decade he also produced many little drawings in black and coloured chalks on brown paper (cf. Plate XII), as well as etchings, drypoints and, after 1878, lithographs. His virtuosity as a decorator is demonstrated in the 'Peacock Room' (cf. Fig. 3), which he designed for a wealthy, but not wholly appreciative, London patron; and his interest in the art of design appears in a working collaboration with the architect Edward William Godwin.

In 1877 an intemperate attack by the critic John Ruskin on The Falling Rocket (Plate XI) – 'flinging a pot of paint in the public's face' – forced Whistler into a libel action. The financial result – Whistler was awarded a farthing's damages and no costs – combined with other debts to leave him bankrupt. Moreover, the opposition of one so influential as Ruskin made the buying of his work a far from respectable business. After spending the year 1879-80 in Venice, he returned to London and prepared to fight his way back to acceptance.

In later life Whistler continued to paint his formal portrait Arrangements, complementing them with small intimate portraits and interiors. The Nocturnes, however, were mostly replaced by little sea-scapes, landscapes and town-scapes.

In 1885 he defined his ideas as an artist in his 'Ten O'Clock' lecture which contains passages that read almost like a defence of abstract art. A retrospective exhibition in 1892 was a great success and, having at last re-conquered London, he and his wife moved to Paris where they lived until 1895. The blow of his wife's death in 1896 and his own ill health clouded his last years and increased his contentiousness. His art, however, never became stale. Until his death on July 17, 1903, he continued to produce an unbroken sequence of paintings, pastels, watercolours, etchings and lithographs to which he gave as much thought as at any time in his career.

'If Velázquez had painted our river he would have painted it something in this style.' —The *Times* art critic

on a painting by Whistler, 1864

rejected the direct contact with nature out of which Monet's Impressionism was born.

At first it was the art and the example of Ingres, that great opposite of Courbet, that he hoped would come to his rescue. But three years of uncertainty and frustration were to show that, for him, true guidance was not from that source. When, with the portrait of his mother, 1871-72 (Louvre, Paris), with *Thomas Carlyle* (Cover Plate) and *Miss Cicely Alexander* (Plate IX), he emerged secure and self-confident, the inspiration and help had come from Velázquez. And so it was to remain for the rest of his life. The *Times* critic wrote more truly than he could possibly have known. His words about a painting made when Whistler was still in his twenties define a relationship constant in all his art.

WHISTLER'S LIFE was one of recurrent removals. America, Russia, France, England — by the time he was thirty he had lived in all these countries; and though, from about 1860 onwards, his address was mostly in England, London became a base rather than a home. He was for ever on the move, not only to other places and other countries, but so frequently from house to house that his friends came to accept the packing cases in his front hall as perfectly natural. The rootlessness of his life is perhaps the key to an understanding of him as an artist. American by birth, he had no contact with and no knowledge of his American contemporaries except for his fellow expatriates, Mary Cassatt and John Singer Sargent; English by long residence he refused to be assimilated by those whom, to the end, he called 'The Islanders'; and if, as is sometimes implied, France was his spiritual home, why did he separate himself from it physically and, in his art, stylistically?

In Paris in the 1850's Whistler, like others of his generation, fell under the spell of Courbet. Even before being introduced to him he must have known his work well. The 'French Set' etchings (or, to use the original, highly appropriate title, 'Twelve Etchings from Nature'), which had been made a few months earlier, adhere closely to the doctrine of Realism; and his first independent paintings— of an old flower-seller, of a man with a pipe between

A T FIRST READING, the words quoted above seem scarcely to apply to Whistler. Dandy, wit, controversialist, painter of refined pictures signed with an elegant butterfly emblem—how can he be compared with that great and most deliberate master of the direct statement? For many years the most commonly accepted conception of Whistler—one which his own conversation and many of his own actions did much to foster—has been as a gifted artist who was content to put taste above creative power. John Rewald, historian of Impressionism, summed up this view. 'By turning his back to nature,' Mr. Rewald wrote, 'by ignoring Courbet's message, Whistler henceforth condemned himself never to penetrate beneath the surface of appearances, to be satisfied with decorative arrangements.' If nineteenth-century art is to be measured, as it so often is, by the yardstick of Impressionism this is a natural, perhaps even an inevitable, assessment. Whistler can be seen as one who had all the advantages of a good education, and yet failed to make use of them.

At the beginning of his career he had been at the very centre of the *avant-garde*. In Fantin-Latour's *Hommage à Delacroix* of 1864 (Louvre, Paris) he stands prominently among such men of progress as Bracquemond, Manet, Baudelaire, Champfleury and Duranty. He was the protégé and friend of Courbet and, in 1865, was his companion on a painting expedition to Trouville. Daubigny and Monet, another master-pupil combination, were also there. They were painting sea-scapes and their association could scarcely have been closer. Yet when Whistler returned to London he was to turn against the things he had shared with the three French artists. By a conscious effort of will, and not without much anguished deliberation, he

2. SAN BIAGIO
*One of the 'Twenty-six
etchings of Venice' 1880*

his teeth, and of a peasant woman—are, if anything, more proletarian and more austere than those of his master. But Whistler tended to avoid commitment to any one movement. The West Point side of his nature could never have accepted Courbet's socialism. His Realism, like that of Manet, for the most part, and like that of the critics Duranty and Austruc, must have always been apolitical. And he was too ardent in his pursuit of progress to be an over-loyal conformist of any kind. Towards the end of his life Degas is reported to have said: 'In our beginnings Fantin, Whistler and I were all on the same road, the road from Holland.' It is easy to see how naturally Whistler's enthusiasm for Rembrandt and Hals, and for the Dutch painters of domestic interiors, led to his espousal of Courbet's cause. But in these apprentice years there was another and ultimately more profound influence. As early as 1857, in the company of a fellow student at Gleyre's, he made a journey to Manchester to see the fourteen paintings by, or attributed to, Velázquez in the Art Treasures exhibition. It must, for Whistler, have been a decisive visit: if the stimulus for his work came from the example of Courbet, it was to be sustained by the more detached art of Velázquez.

W HISTLER'S FIRST major painting, *At the Piano* (Plate I), is surely the one Degas had most immediately in mind when he wrote of 'the road from Holland'. In contrast with the early figure pictures it is constructed with extreme deliberation. As in a painting by Vermeer or Pieter de Hooch, the two figures are in profile and set against a wall broken into geometrical shapes by the pictures which hang on it. But however Dutch the inspiration (and it is surely significant that, in 1867, Thoré-Bürger, the French critic who re-discovered Vermeer, made enquiries about buying it), there is nothing of pastiche. This is a mid-nineteenth-century picture—though more austere than most. If some of its elements come from sources other than Courbet, there are as yet none in opposition to the ideas on which Courbet's work is based.

Although much of Whistler's later development is fore-shadowed in the paintings and etchings he made during the three or four years after his arrival in London, there was at first no sudden change of style. Pictures such as *The Thames in Ice* (Plate II) are still inspired by the world of Courbet; and the choice of the Thames and the industrial landscape of the London docks for several paintings and the sixteen etchings of the 'Thames Set' is well in keeping with the tenets of Realism. But already Whistler was preparing to free himself from this doctrine. In *The Thames in Ice*, except for its remarkably free brushwork, there are few innovations. But in its successor *Wapping* (Collection of Mr. and Mrs. John Hay Whitney, Manhasset, N.Y.), at which he worked and reworked during the years 1860 to 1864, the conscious process of arrangement, already apparent in *At the Piano*, was carried further. For Whistler the answer to problems of composition came, not from Courbet, nor even from Vermeer, but from Velázquez. It is therefore not extraordinary that, at a time when the intended relationship of the figures to the background in *Wapping* continued to elude him, he should, in the autumn of 1862, have decided to make the visit to the Prado which, in the past, he had so often postponed. Near Biarritz, still on the French side of the Pyrenees, he hesitated. Fantin, who was to join him, could not get away from Paris, and the visit was put off, as it happened, for ever. The image of Velázquez was to remain, not sharply through detailed study but as a source of remote power. This was perhaps subconsciously the way Whistler wanted it. Too complete an absorption in Courbet had already threatened his own independence; in the Prado he might have been overwhelmed.

The product of the halted excursion to Madrid was *The Blue Wave, Biarritz* (Plate III), a work of remarkable boldness and directness. But this picture was not, at least not for a long time, to herald a new and freer attitude to landscape. First, Pre-Raphaelitism—to which Whistler's friendship with Rossetti and Swinburne had introduced him—was to lead his art in a very different direction. *The White Girl*, later *Symphony in White, No. 1* (Plate IV), though devoid of the literary associations nearly always present in the works of the members of the Brotherhood, has something of their delicate melancholy. Even when, in about 1863, Whistler became a devotee of all things Oriental, the consequent 'Japanese' pictures were really Pre-Raphaelite works in fancy dress. The pose of *La Princesse du Pays de la Porcelaine* (Plate V) may derive from the tradition of Harunobu, the eighteenth-century Japanese painter; but the adaptation of the Japanese costume to Western standards of comfort, the cosy setting of Chinese screen, carpet and vase, and the wistful Victorianism of the girl's expression are completely occidental. In his second white symphony, *The Little White Girl* (Plate VIII), in which an English girl leans on a European mantel-shelf and only the accessories are of the East, Whistler himself seems to admit that, between his Pre-Raphaelitism and his *Japonerie*, the differences in mood and spirit are incidental and superficial.

The relationship of figure to reflection in *The Little White Girl* suggests that Whistler was well aware of Ingres's preoccupation with the same problem in pictures like his *Portrait of the Comtesse d'Haussonville* of 1845 (Frick Collection, New York). Indeed, in the later 1860's, Ingres was very much in his thoughts. In a letter to Fantin he wrote, 'I like his pictures only moderately . . . But if only I had been his pupil what a teacher he would have been! How he would have guided us sanely!' Ingres's unerring draughtsmanship would, he felt, have provided him with the missing ingredient for the reconciliation of line, colour and form that he was seeking. As it was, things refused to come right; and the addition of new, and not very reconcilable, elements led to a kind of artificiality. Without discarding his Orientalism he was led by the example of an English friend, the likeable but minor painter Albert Moore, to seek academic discipline by giving his figures the classical forms of the Greek statuettes from Tanagra. His whole temperament, however, was against the task he had set himself. The period, 1866 to 1870, became one of incompletely realized projects and unfinished pictures. In a work like *Variations in Blue and Green* (Plate VII) there is, despite the immense thought that went into its making, the freshness of a sketch. But when he went further the result seems over-laborious, and the large *Three Figures: Pink and Grey* of 1868-69 (Tate Gallery, London) is a comparative failure.

WHISTLER'S REGAINED self-reliance in the 1870's was born out of everything that had gone before—the failures no less than the successes. In the Nocturnes of the Thames and Chelsea, the Realism of his early work and the aestheticism of his reaction against it are effectively fused into a harmonious relationship of form and colour which, however arbitrary it became, still takes its reference from nature. The dissolving silhouettes of the Nocturne of *Old Battersea Bridge* (Plate X) are unmistakably those of London's riverside; and, for all the abstraction, the scene of *The Falling Rocket* (Plate XI) is still that of a Chelsea amusement park. The excursion into an artificial world of Japanese girls and cherry blossom, of gracefully-poised Greek figures in diaphanous drapery, was not all loss. But in the Nocturnes and, perhaps even more so, in the portrait Arrangements, Whistler found that his inspiration had to be based on something more real. In a picture like the famous portrait of the artist's mother, *Arrangement in Grey and Black, No. 1*, c. 1871 (Louvre, Paris), and its skilfully varied male counterpart, *Thomas Carlyle* (Cover Plate), boldness and inevitability replace the uncertainties of the Greco-Japanese figure pieces. The

early lessons from Courbet and the Dutch masters are put to good use. But, above all, the mood of the Arrangements is the mood of Velázquez. The little Miss Cicely Alexander in *Harmony in Grey and Green* (Plate IX), though dressed in the clothes of the mid-nineteenth-century, has all the haughty elegance of a Spanish Infanta.

When in 1877 Ruskin made his notorious 'pot-of-paint' attack, Whistler was forty-three. For years everything had gone well for him: he was satisfied with his own work and sales and commissions were good. His brilliantly inventive decoration of the Peacock Room, 1876-77 (reconstructed in the Freer Gallery, Washington, D.C., see Fig. 3), with an attenuated pattern anticipating the motifs of Art Nouveau, was the art talk of London. He had himself become a patron of architecture, commissioning his friend E. W. Godwin to design the White House for him in a style as advanced as his own. In 1879 the security that lay behind this success was removed. In his bankruptcy sales all his pictures not stored with friends, and all his Japanese prints and Chinese porcelain, were sold. The newly occupied White House had to go — most gallingly to a critic for whom Whistler had nothing but contempt. The blow was a devastating one.

It has been argued—with only superficial justification —that Ruskin's attack and the humiliation that followed it were to bring out an extreme aggressiveness in Whistler the man and to stifle his creativity as an artist. It is true that as he got older he became increasingly touchy and quarrelsome. It is also true that in his art after 1880 there are no spectacular innovations to match, say, the invention of the Nocturnes. But at no time did he ever become self-satisfied. Within a year of his bankruptcy he was producing little pastels of Venice, like *Red and Gold: Salute, Sunset* (Plate XII), whose glowing colours anticipate Monet's Venetian pictures of the first decade of the twentieth century. For the most part, however, his later art is a development—perhaps (with no pejorative meaning) a refinement—of certain of his earlier styles. The large portrait Arrangements of his maturity and old age conform to an already evolved pattern: but they are miraculously un-

3. STUDY OF PEACOCKS FOR THE 'PEACOCK ROOM' c. 1876
Birnie Philip Gift, University Art Collection, Glasgow

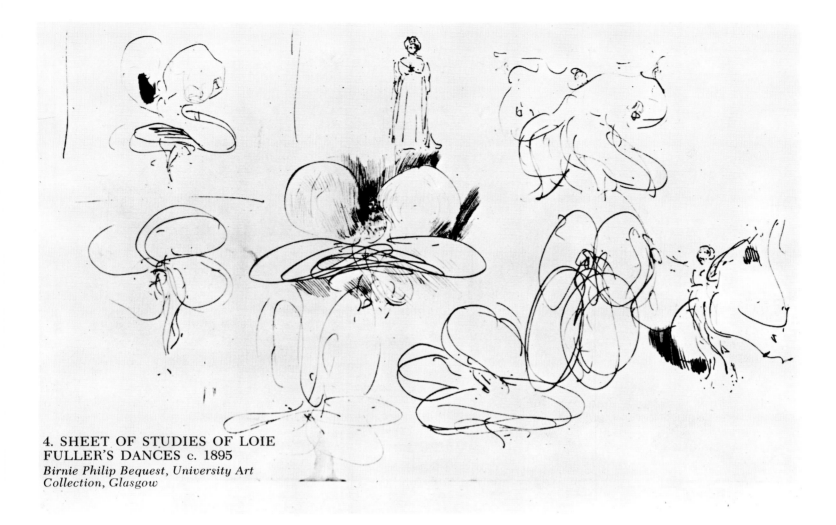

4. SHEET OF STUDIES OF LOIE
FULLER'S DANCES c. 1895
*Birnie Philip Bequest, University Art
Collection, Glasgow*

repetitive—ranging from the stately elegance of *Lady Meux* (Plate XIII) to the drama of *Sarasate* of 1884 (Carnegie Institute, Pittsburgh) and the bravado of a last self-portrait, *Gold and Brown,* 1898-1903 (Birnie Philip Gift, University Art Collection, Glasgow), in the pose of a Velázquez *bufón.* Their informal counterparts, especially those of children and young models like *Dorothy Seton* (Plate XVI), have at their best an immediacy and a freshness not previously achieved. In landscape, there are, after 1880, no more of the Thames Nocturnes. But water—sea, estuary, river and canal—continued to fascinate Whistler: one of his very last paintings was of a tumultuous sea, a kind of miniature *Blue Wave* (Plate III) rendered in skeletal form.

IF IN WHISTLER'S later art there is a quality of recapitulation, there are also elements that are new. In some ways he seems to have more in common with the younger progressives of the 1890's than he ever had with his contemporaries, the Impressionists. He collected Art Nouveau prints, was a subscriber to the Austrian Secession periodical 'Ver Sacrum' and, in a sheet of drawings of Loie Fuller (Fig. 4), made a personal excursion into the style of this movement. An affinity with Bonnard and Vuillard is also discernible: little cigar-box-size portraits like *L'Écharpe Rose* (Plate XV) and paintings with minute full-length figures in domestic settings have much of the character of these artists' *intimisme.* But it is, perhaps, in the face-on shop front pictures, produced in almost endless succession during the last twenty years of his life, that Whistler was most prophetically modern. In them the geometrical backgrounds of works like *At the Piano* and *Thomas Carlyle* are, as it were, given separate existence. At the Ruskin trial Whistler had said of *The Falling Rocket:* 'I have per-

haps meant to indicate an artistic interest alone in my work, divesting the picture from any outside sort of interest which might have been otherwise attached to it. It is an arrangement of line, form and colour first. . . .' The words apply with even more exactness to *Green and Gold: a Shop in Calais* (Plate XIV), in which the interrelation of verticals and horizontals is carried almost to the threshold of abstraction.

DID WHISTLER, as Mr. Rewald has it, reject the inspiration of nature and thereby condemn himself 'never to penetrate beneath the surface of appearances'? The question, with the implication it contains, does not really make sense. It is—to refer to an older battle of styles—like reproving Poussin because he did not paint like Rubens. Whistler's repudiation of Courbet's Realism was not some kind of aberration: it was the inevitable consequence of a process of self-realization. Because his beginnings were so similar to those of the Impressionists he well understood what they were doing. But his own aim, sometimes imperfectly achieved, was to find a more ruminative mode of expression. He did not seek a direct rendering of natural appearances; but, despite his theoretical arguments, his abstract titles, and the geometrical disciplining of his compositions, he remained a painter of recognizable people and recognizable places. He approached abstraction; but it was a decade or so after his death before a truly abstract picture was to be painted. Perhaps his place between those who expound nature and those who withdraw from it is not unlike Velázquez's between *Rubenisme* and *Poussinisme.* Whistler himself would certainly have welcomed any comparison that linked his name with that of the master of Madrid.

I. AT THE PIANO (1859)
Oil on canvas. 26 in. x 35⅛ in.
Taft Museum, Cincinnati

This, the artist's first major painting, reflects the influence of the Dutch 17th-century masters Whistler studied and admired. At the same time, however, it has elements characteristic of many of his later works: his preference for black and white and generally low-keyed colours, his fondness for a horizontal line across the canvas and for silhouetted figures, his decorative use of picture frames.

The figures of Mrs. Haden, Whistler's half-sister, and her daughter Annie provide the strongest colour contrasts. The warm maroon of the carpet and covered table serves as an effective base for these dramatic black and white masses. Though dark hues predominate—in the rich black of Mrs. Haden's dress and the reddish browns of the piano—the gold and white of the pictures, the pale green wall and the decorative moldings lighten the work, while adding geometric interest.

Rejected by the 1859 Salon in Paris, the painting was hung in the British Royal Academy in 1860 and was subsequently purchased by an academician. Because most English painting of the day was sentimental, Whistler's realism and simplicity were rejected by critics. Yet his work was admired by other artists, who praised his fluid technique and austere composition.

II. THE THAMES IN ICE (1860–61)
Oil on canvas. 29⅝ in. x 21¾ in.
Smithsonian Institution, Freer Gallery of Art, Washington, D.C.

Painted after Whistler finally settled in London, this painting and other works in 'the Thames set' show the artist's fascination with life along the river. The French realist influence is much in evidence, but the treatment of the distant factories, the sky and the water foreshadows the evocative mood of the later Nocturnes. Beginning to free his brushwork and simplify his forms, Whistler was on the verge of forsaking Realism for a freer, more dynamic and abstract technique.

The boats here are rendered with an almost dry brush over a thinly painted background. The masts and sails are accurately drawn, not merely suggested, as they would be in later river paintings. The heavy impasto of the snowy foreground and the ice floes in the background is reminiscent of Courbet's similar treatment. Whistler's beiges, browns, whites and greys illustrate the artist's continued preference for the monochromatic, yet the variations within these colours give the work richness and complexity.

III. BLUE AND SILVER: THE BLUE WAVE, BIARRITZ (1862)
Oil on canvas. 24½ in. x 34½ in.
Hill-Stead Museum, Farmington, Connecticut

In the autumn of 1862, Whistler set out with his mistress, Jo Heffernan, for southern France and Spain. On this journey he hoped to recover from a bout of painter's colic, brought on by inhaling toxic fumes of white lead during the previous winter's work on *Symphony in White, No. 1* (Plate IV), and also to study the Velázquez portraits in the Prado in Madrid. In the course of their travels they stopped on the French coast near Biarritz. Fascinated by water throughout his life, Whistler sought in this vigourous seascape to capture the angry Atlantic in its elemental force and majesty.

Influenced by his mentor Courbet, Whistler painted *Blue and Silver* directly from nature, using a thick impasto to achieve forms of realistic strength and solidity. But, already diverging from the imitative, detailed approach of realist painters, he simplified the scene in an effort to seize a single fleeting moment in his observation of sky and water. Discarding most of the modelling and line he had used in earlier works, he preferred here to suggest the forms of rocks, waves and clouds by patchily applied pigment and thin, flat brush strokes. In later paintings this technique was to become even sketchier and more spontaneous, like that of the Impressionists, who were leading French art in new directions.

IV. SYMPHONY IN WHITE, NO. 1: THE WHITE GIRL (1862)

Oil on canvas. 85½ in. x 43 in.
National Gallery of Art, Washington, D.C.
(Harris Whittemore Collection)

During the 1860's, Whistler frequently painted Jo Heffernan, the handsome, dignified, Irish-born model who shared his life for about ten years. Here he dressed her in soft white cambric, with her long auburn hair unbound, and posed her on a white bearskin against a white curtain, staring off into space. The figure, atmospherically silhouetted against a blank background, suggests the influence of Velázquez. The purposely unfashionable, romantic effect, combined with Jo's melancholy expression, was reminiscent of the aestheticism of D.G. Rossetti and other Pre-Raphaelites. But unlike their works and those of the academicians, Whistler's *White Girl,* as the painting was first called, was not intended to tell a story. In response to queries about its meaning, Whistler declared, 'My painting simply represents a girl dressed in white, standing in front of a white curtain'.

Although the work was poorly understood and aroused much controversy, it was praised by a few perceptive artists who admired the relationships of its subtle whites, and one critic called it a 'symphony in white'. Whistler later adopted this phrase as the new title of the picture, using it again for two other portraits. In these and other works, in which subject matter was increasingly only a means of exploring relationships of tone and space, Whistler was moving towards the credo of modern art—art for art's sake.

V. ROSE AND SILVER: LA PRINCESSE DU PAYS DE LA PORCELAINE (1864)

Oil on canvas. 78¾ in. x 45¾ in.

Smithsonian Institution, Freer Gallery of Art, Washington, D.C.

Shortly after Whistler encountered the Pre-Raphaelites he discovered Oriental art, especially Chinese blue-and-white porcelain and Japanese woodcuts, which were becoming fashionable in avant-garde circles. With characteristic enthusiasm for the new and exotic, he incorporated Oriental motifs in his works. He asked Christine Spartali, beautiful daughter of his friend the Greek consul general in London, to wear a Japanese kimono and hold a fan for the portrait titled *Rose and Silver*. Her pose is derived from that of an 18th-century Japanese courtesan, and a Chinese rug and screen contribute to the Oriental effect. Christine's face and hair, however, are in the Pre-Raphaelite style, and the crowded, decorative setting tends to suggest a Victorian parlour.

Christine's father, dismayed at seeing his daughter in costume and disliking the painter's prominent signature in the upper left-hand corner, declined to purchase the work. Eventually it was bought by Whistler's patron, the Liverpool shipowner F. R. Leyland, who hung it in the dining room of his new London house. Leyland had the room decorated to fit the portrait and his porcelain collection, but Whistler objected to the result and insisted on making changes. In the process he created the famous 'Peacock Room' (1876–77), over which he and Leyland ultimately quarrelled.

VI. SYMPHONY IN GREY AND GREEN: THE OCEAN
(1866)
Oil on canvas. 31¼ in. x 39 in.
Frick Collection, New York

In 1866 Whistler made a brief trip to Chile. During his stay in Valparaiso, the artist painted this picture and five other seascapes from a window overlooking the harbour.

The composition of these works reflects Whistler's growing selectivity as he omitted more and more details to create the desired Oriental space. Perhaps because of their greater simplicity, he was more successful at sustaining the Japanese mood in his seascapes and river pictures than in his figure compositions.

Here, the quiet waters of the harbour are rendered in thin, luminous strips of lavender, soft green and bluish grey. Bright daubs of white pigment within these luminous greys show the artist's increasing freedom in depicting water (cf. Plate III). The hazy forms of ships lying at anchor are captured with quick, delicate strokes. The pier at the left, with its carefully drawn pilings, is the most literally portrayed element in the picture. Together with the subtly brushed branches in the lower right foreground it helps to break up the expanse of water. The small rectangle at the extreme right contains Whistler's famous 'butterfly signature', in this instance made to resemble the ideograms of Japanese printmakers.

VII. VARIATIONS IN BLUE AND GREEN (*c.* 1868–69)
Oil on prepared board mounted on wood.
18½ in. x 24½ in.
Smithsonian Institution, Freer Gallery of Art, Washington, D.C.

The late 1860's were a difficult period for Whistler as he sought to find his personal style as an artist. He began a number of ambitious figure compositions in which he combined Pre-Raphaelite, Japanese and classical Greek influences. In *Variations in Blue and Green*, the figure on the left, gracefully leaning on one hip, was inspired by one of the Hellenistic terra-cotta figurines in Whistler's collection. Her flowing ochre and lavender drapery, suggested by strong directional brush strokes resembling finger painting, enhances the curved line of her pose. Completely different in feeling are the concealing green and lavender robes of the bending figures on the right, derived from Japanese woodcuts.

Whistler was unable, however, to complete these works to his satisfaction. He blamed his failure on his insufficient academic art training, particularly regretting that he had not studied with Ingres, the early 19th-century master of classical draftsmanship. Eventually the uncompleted oil sketches, called the Six Projects, were bought by his American patron Charles Freer. To 20th-century eyes, their sketchy quality seems to convey the artist's intentions as well as the most meticulous old-master drawings.

VIII. SYMPHONY IN WHITE, NO. 2:
    THE LITTLE WHITE GIRL (1864) — *Detail*
    Oil on canvas. 30 in. x 20 in.
    Tate Gallery, London

In his second 'symphony in white' Whistler again used his mistress Jo Heffernan as a model and continued to investigate the relationship of pale tones. The heavy impasto technique with which he rendered her white dress carries over from the influence of Courbet. Jo's flowing hair and idealized pensive expression (unlike her natural good spirits) reveal the lingering attraction of Pre-Raphaelitism.

The juxtaposition of the figure leaning against the mantelpiece with her reflection in the glass above indicates that Whistler was familiar with the treatment of the reflected image by such painters as Rubens, Velázquez and Ingres. The atmosphere of calm suggests the orderly interiors painted by 17th-century Dutch masters, whom he had admired from his student days. Whistler embellished the portrait with the tips of flowering sprays, a scarlet lacquer bowl, a blue-and-white porcelain vase and the fan which Jo holds in her right hand (not visible here). These motifs are evidence of the artist's new enthusiasm for exotic eastern objects before he had begun to really assimilate the formal aspects of Oriental style.

The painting was exhibited at the Royal Academy and inspired the poet Swinburne to write a complimentary poem. Later in Paris it received the Grand Prix.

IX. HARMONY IN GREY AND GREEN: MISS CICELY ALEXANDER (1872–73)
Oil on canvas. 74¾ in. x 38½ in.
Tate Gallery, London

Whistler's feeling for children is demonstrated by this enchanting portrait. He made elaborate preparations for the work, first selecting the muslin for the little girl's dress, then supervising its execution and even specifying how it was to be laundered. The design on the floor was also carefully planned: Whistler had strips of black and white tape sewn together to produce the precise effect he wanted.

Nine-year-old Cicely Alexander, the daughter of one of Whistler's early patrons, posed for some seventy sittings, each one lasting for several hours. Years later, she said that she had regarded herself as something of a victim through all of this, and, indeed, Whistler caught a rather pouting expression on her dainty face. She stands, quite formally, at a three-quarter angle to the viewer, with an elegantly plumed hat in her left hand. Whistler's subtle handling of the sheer white material of her dress, enhanced by the silvery grey of the overskirt, is further emphasized by the muted colouring of the wall behind her. This flat background, barely differentiated from the plane of the floor, has a strongly Oriental flavour that derives chiefly from the screenlike linear quality of the black dado and detail strip. Also suggesting the Japanese influence are the tall daisies peeping into the right edge of the canvas and the delicate butterflies hovering above the subject (echoed by the Whistler butterfly monogram at centre left).

X. NOCTURNE IN BLUE AND GOLD: OLD BATTERSEA BRIDGE (c. 1872–75)

Oil on canvas. 26½ in. x 19¾ in.
Tate Gallery, London

While the Impressionists struggled to represent the effects of sunlight on the Seine, Whistler was painting nighttime scenes inspired by nocturnal boat trips on the Thames and rambles through Chelsea, where he had his studio. On these excursions he took no colour notes. If he could not visualize the effect the next day in his studio, he returned to the same place the following night to refresh his memory. He intended the Nocturnes not to represent specific sites, such as the Old Battersea Bridge in this work, but to convey the mood created by the dim, blurred forms and dark, subdued tones of night. When asked whether the blobs on the bridge were figures, he replied, 'They are just what you like. The picture is simply a representation of moonlight'.

Working on an especially absorbent canvas prepared with a red ground to bring up the predominant blues of the Nocturnes, Whistler used his highly personal vision to create images that are both evocative and daring. The vast, misty blue spaces of sky and water are brightened by the lights and spatter of fireworks from the pleasure grounds of Cremorne Gardens. These open areas are set off by the strong, dark, vertical pier of the bridge, balanced by the three lighter horizontals formed by the bridge railing, the shore on the horizon and a barge in the foreground. In such an asymmetrical balance of forms and voids, Whistler went far beyond the superficial inclusion of Oriental motifs in earlier works to a deeper appreciation of the Japanese sense of composition.

XI. NOCTURNE IN BLACK AND GOLD: THE FALLING ROCKET (*c.* 1874)
Oil on wood. 23¾ in. x 18¾ in.
Detroit Institute of Arts

In this most brilliantly innovative of his Nocturnes, Whistler set down his unique impression of the light, forms and atmosphere of a passing moment in Thamesside London at night. Most of the panel is occupied by a sky of velvety blue-blacks thinned with transparent blue-grey washes and spangled with impasto dots of pure white and yellow suggesting the fireworks of Cremorne Gardens, a popular amusement park. In the middle distance, forms that may be buildings are dimly illuminated by the light of exploding rockets. Indistinct, vaguely human figures hold the foreground. Of all Whistler's work, this example departs furthest from the realistic representation of nature that the public expected.

When the eminent critic John Ruskin, who fervently believed in the obligation of art to uphold morality, saw *Nocturne in Black and Gold* on exhibition in 1877, he was outraged. In a magazine article he criticized Whistler for flinging 'a pot of paint in the public's face' and then having the audacity to charge 200 guineas for it. Incensed at this attack by an avowed enemy of 'art for art's sake', Whistler sued Ruskin for libel.

At the trial neither judge nor jury appreciated the significance of the plaintiff's statement that the painting was not a view of Cremorne but merely 'an artistic arrangement'. Although the verdict was in Whistler's favour, only token damages were awarded and the judge ordered both men to split the court costs. The burden of this expense, added to Whistler's other considerable debts, left him bankrupt.

XII. RED AND GOLD: SALUTE, SUNSET (1880)
Pastel on brown paper. 8 in. x 12 in.
University of Glasgow

During his year in Venice (1879–80), Whistler produced more than fifty pastels and forty etchings. In both these media he simplified his forms and became increasingly freer in his style. Although he had worked relatively little in pastels heretofore, he appreciated the kind of visual shorthand they afforded. Riding in a gondola, he would ask the gondolier to stop at a promising spot, and he would quickly capture the essence of a particular view. For drawing he used full sticks of pastel and for blending, the soft bluntness of broken pieces. Whistler's sensitive and economical application of colour in this medium represents a radical departure from the realistic method advocated by such artists as Manet and Fantin-Latour, which was far tighter and less sketchy. Because of the fragility of pastels, once a picture was completed, he protected it between sheets of silver-coated paper. Thus, curiously enough, many of these works have retained their delicate, fresh colour even more than his oils.

Here, the shadowy blue silhouette of the Church of the Salute floats on a pearly white and blue indication of the lagoon. A few streaks of red, gold and pink are enough to suggest the sunset in this fleeting impression evoking the romance and mystery of Venice.

XIII. HARMONY IN PINK AND GREY: LADY MEUX
(1881)
Oil on canvas. 75¼ in. x 36½ in.
Frick Collection, New York

Whistler's later portraits, like his Nocturnes, continued to be primarily arrangements of forms and colours He did two portraits of the shapely, black-eyed Valerie, Lady Meux, a former barmaid at the Gaiety Theatre, who had become the elegant wife of a rich brewer. The first, *Arrangement in White and Black*, so pleased the sitter that she ordered a second. In *Harmony in Pink and Grey*, the narrow, upright figure in silhouette still follows the precedent set by Velázquez, but it stands in the fashionable S-curve achieved by the bustle dress of that day. The rosy greys of Lady Meux' costume and the curtain behind her are further warmed by her pink bodice and ruffles, brushed with bravura strokes of white to bring out the sheen of the satin, and by the soft red carpet at her feet.

This work was admired at the Paris Salon of 1892, and Whistler then began a third portrait. But his sharp tongue, which, along with his refusal to flatter, tended to deter fashionable sitters, led to Lady Meux' hasty departure from his studio. The third portrait was never completed.

XIV. GREEN AND GOLD: A SHOP IN CALAIS
(c. 1892–1900)
Oil on wood. 8½ in. x 5 in.
University of Glasgow
(Birnie Philip Gift)

While working in Venice, Whistler caught the atmosphere of that ancient city in delicate etchings and sketchy yet evocative pastels. His interest in atmosphere and the formal elements of line, tone and texture carried over into the spontaneous small oil landscapes and townscapes of his later years.

In *Green and Gold*, he treated the oil paint like a colour wash, enabling him to set down with immediacy his impression of a time-worn, weather-beaten channel port. The muted, rain-streaked colours of this Calais shopfront, with its dark, empty door and windows, convey an air of mystery and mellow decay. The verticals and horizontals combine to represent a still recognizable subject. But Whistler's interest in them as geometric elements of composition foreshadows the Neoplasticism of Mondrian, whose reduction of painting to nonobjective varieties of grids opened a new age in modern art.

XV. L'ÉCHARPE ROSE (*c.* 1892–95)
Oil on wood. 10⅛ in. x 7⅛ in.
University of Glasgow
(Birnie Philip Gift)

Living happily in Paris in the early 1890's with his wife Trixie, Whistler painted two portraits of an unknown French girl. The poses are similar, but this painting shows just the head and torso while the other, *Rose et Argent: La Jolie Mutine* (University of Glasgow), is full length.

Here the sensitive melancholy in the sitter's dark eyes, skillfully modelled face and drooping mouth is reminiscent of the sympathetic portrayal of Paris shop girls and entertainers by Degas and Toulouse-Lautrec. Indeed, the freedom and virtuosity with which Whistler handled the girl's gossamer pink scarf or shawl suggests their rapid, sketchy technique. But the soft rosy-violet tones of the face and scarf, echoed in the background, create a subtle harmonic unity that is entirely Whistler's own.

XVI. DOROTHY SETON, A DAUGHTER OF EVE
(1902)
Oil on canvas. 20¼ in. x 12½ in.
University of Glasgow
(Birnie Philip Gift)

This fresh, appealing picture, done the year before Whistler died, shows that his artistic powers were as acute and vigourous as ever. Though he was ill and had to force himself to continue working, many of his late works convey a sense of lively virtuosity.

After showing this portrait to a visitor, Whistler said, 'Most people think she isn't pretty but I feel hers is a remarkable face'. With her red hair and oval face she reminded Whistler of Hogarth's *Shrimp Girl*, at the National Gallery in London. She also bore a strong resemblance to Jo Heffernan and Maud Franklin, Whistler's former companions. The artist claimed he had completed the work in two hours, and it does have the immediacy of a quick oil sketch, with a warmth and sensuosity not often discernible in his earlier work. That Whistler felt a special attraction to this model is suggested by her holding an apple, symbol of Eve's temptation. Here there is no wan elegance but an earthy portrayal, without pretense.